# *My* CHEERLEADING *Season*

A journal of my skills,
my games, and my memories.

## Karleen Tauszik

Published by Tip Top Books, Dunedin, Florida

Text and layout copyright © 2021 by Karleen Tauszik
Cover Illustration from BigstockPhoto.com, photo 8091994, contributor Penywise.
Cover Design Copyright © 2021 by Karleen Tauszik
Cover design and cover photo editing by Karleen Tauszik

All rights reserved, including the right of reproduction in whole or in part in any form.

Summary: This journal provides children and teens with a place to track their cheerleading season: their games, practices, areas of improvement and contribution, and their fun memories.

ISBN-13: 978-1-954130-13-5

Karleen Tauszik is the author of books for children ages 8-12. Visit her on the web at KarleenT.com, where you can see her other books and sign up for her newsletter.

This book belongs to

My Cheerleading Season

from _____ to _____
	Date	Date

## Hurrah! You're on the squad!

This journal is the perfect place to track your cheerleading season—your practice sessions, your games, the highlights of the season, and all the fun you'll have.

Here's what you'll find inside:

First, there are 6 pages to journal your pre-season weeks of practice.

Next, there are enough pages to journal up to 20 games, so you have enough for preseason games, the main season, and a few for tournaments. Need more? One is reserved for photocopying.

In between each game page, you'll find a page to journal how your practice sessions are going.

At the end, there are seven blank pages to fill with photos, extra notes, and mementos. You can even get the other cheerleaders to write notes and their autographs if you like. Add whatever you want to so you remember your cheering season and make this book uniquely yours.

Good luck and have a great season!

# Pre-Season Practice

The week starting
Day & Date

The main things we're focusing on this week are:

My focus this week is:

How I feel starting out:

What I think I can contribute to the squad this week:

My notes about this week's practice:

# Pre-Season Practice

The week starting _____
Day & Date

The main things we're focusing on this week are: _____

My focus this week is: _____

How I feel starting out: _____

What I think I can contribute to the squad this week: _____

My notes about this week's practice: _____

# Pre-Season Practice

The week starting _____
                    Day & Date

The main things we're focusing on this week are: _____

My focus this week is: _____

How I feel starting out: _____

What I think I can contribute to the squad this week: _____

My notes about this week's practice: _____

# Pre-Season Practice

The week starting _____
Day & Date

The main things we're focusing on this week are:


My focus this week is:


How I feel starting out:


What I think I can contribute to the squad this week:


My notes about this week's practice:

# Pre-Season Practice

The week starting _____
Day & Date

The main things we're focusing on this week are: _____

_____

_____

My focus this week is: _____

_____

_____

How I feel starting out: _____

_____

_____

What I think I can contribute to the squad this week: _____

_____

_____

My notes about this week's practice: _____

_____

_____

_____

_____

_____

_____

# Pre-Season Practice

The week starting _____
Day & Date

The main things we're focusing on this week are: _____

_____

My focus this week is: _____

_____

How I feel starting out: _____

_____

What I think I can contribute to the squad this week: _____

_____

My notes about this week's practice: _____

_____

# Game Day

Game Date: _____  Game Time: _____

We played against: _____  Home ☐   Away ☐

Final Score: _____

My summary of our cheering performance: _____

_____

_____

_____

Coach's comments: _____

_____

_____

What I did well: _____

_____

_____

_____

Where I could have done better: _____

_____

_____

_____

Highlights of our cheering: _____

_____

_____

_____

Highlights of the game: _____

_____

# Practice

Starting _____ until our next game on _____
              Day & Date                                               Day & Date

The main things we're focusing on this week are: _____

_____

My focus this week is: _____

_____

How I feel looking ahead: _____

_____

What I think I can contribute to the squad this week: _____

_____

My notes about this week's practice: _____

_____

_____

_____

_____

# Game Day

Game Date: _____  Game Time: _____

We played against: _____  Home ☐  Away ☐

Final Score: _____

My summary of our cheering performance:
_____
_____
_____

Coach's comments:
_____
_____

What I did well:
_____
_____
_____

Where I could have done better:
_____
_____
_____

Highlights of our cheering:
_____
_____
_____

Highlights of the game:
_____
_____

# Practice

Starting _____ until our next game on _____
           Day & Date                                            Day & Date

The main things we're focusing on this week are:

My focus this week is:

How I feel looking ahead:

What I think I can contribute to the squad this week:

My notes about this week's practice:

# Game Day

Game Date: _____　　　Game Time: _____

We played against: _____　Home ☐　Away ☐

Final Score: _____

My summary of our cheering performance: _____

_____

_____

Coach's comments: _____

_____

_____

What I did well: _____

_____

_____

Where I could have done better: _____

_____

_____

Highlights of our cheering: _____

_____

_____

Highlights of the game: _____

_____

# Practice

Starting _____ until our next game on _____
               Day & Date                                                                Day & Date

The main things we're focusing on this week are:

My focus this week is:

How I feel looking ahead:

What I think I can contribute to the squad this week:

My notes about this week's practice:

# Game Day

Game Date:                                                    Game Time:

We played against:                                Home ☐    Away ☐

Final Score:

My summary of our cheering performance:

Coach's comments:

What I did well:

Where I could have done better:

Highlights of our cheering:

Highlights of the game:

# Practice

Starting _____ until our next game on _____
                Day & Date                                                               Day & Date

The main things we're focusing on this week are:

My focus this week is:

How I feel looking ahead:

What I think I can contribute to the squad this week:

My notes about this week's practice:

# Game Day

Game Date: _____  Game Time: _____

We played against: _____                Home ☐   Away ☐

Final Score: _____

My summary of our cheering performance:

_____

_____

_____

Coach's comments:

_____

_____

_____

What I did well:

_____

_____

_____

Where I could have done better:

_____

_____

_____

Highlights of our cheering:

_____

_____

_____

Highlights of the game:

_____

_____

# Practice

Starting _____ until our next game on _____
         Day & Date                                 Day & Date

The main things we're focusing on this week are:

My focus this week is:

How I feel looking ahead:

What I think I can contribute to the squad this week:

My notes about this week's practice:

# Game Day

Game Date: _____   Game Time: _____

We played against: _____        Home ☐   Away ☐

Final Score: _____

My summary of our cheering performance: _____

_____
_____
_____

Coach's comments: _____

_____
_____

What I did well: _____

_____
_____
_____

Where I could have done better: _____

_____
_____
_____

Highlights of our cheering: _____

_____
_____
_____

Highlights of the game: _____

_____
_____

# Practice

Starting _____ until our next game on _____
                      Day & Date                                                           Day & Date

The main things we're focusing on this week are:

My focus this week is:

How I feel looking ahead:

What I think I can contribute to the squad this week:

My notes about this week's practice:

# Game Day

Game Date: _____   Game Time: _____

We played against: _____        Home ☐   Away ☐

Final Score: _____

My summary of our cheering performance: _____
_____
_____
_____

Coach's comments: _____
_____
_____

What I did well: _____
_____
_____
_____

Where I could have done better: _____
_____
_____

Highlights of our cheering: _____
_____
_____
_____

Highlights of the game: _____
_____
_____

# Practice

Starting _____ until our next game on _____
                      Day & Date                                                                   Day & Date

The main things we're focusing on this week are: _____

My focus this week is: _____

How I feel looking ahead: _____

What I think I can contribute to the squad this week: _____

My notes about this week's practice: _____

# Game Day

Game Date: _____  Game Time: _____

We played against: _____  Home ☐   Away ☐

Final Score: _____

My summary of our cheering performance:

_____
_____
_____

Coach's comments:

_____
_____
_____

What I did well:

_____
_____
_____

Where I could have done better:

_____
_____
_____

Highlights of our cheering:

_____
_____
_____

Highlights of the game:

_____

# Practice

Starting _____ until our next game on _____
              Day & Date                                                   Day & Date

The main things we're focusing on this week are:

My focus this week is:

How I feel looking ahead:

What I think I can contribute to the squad this week:

My notes about this week's practice:

# Game Day

Game Date: _____  Game Time: _____

We played against: _____  Home ☐   Away ☐

Final Score: _____

My summary of our cheering performance:
_____
_____
_____
_____

Coach's comments:
_____
_____
_____

What I did well:
_____
_____
_____
_____

Where I could have done better:
_____
_____
_____
_____

Highlights of our cheering:
_____
_____
_____
_____

Highlights of the game:
_____
_____

# Practice

Starting _____ until our next game on _____
              Day & Date                                           Day & Date

The main things we're focusing on this week are:

My focus this week is:

How I feel looking ahead:

What I think I can contribute to the squad this week:

My notes about this week's practice:

# Game Day

Game Date: _____   Game Time: _____

We played against: _____   Home ☐   Away ☐

Final Score: _____

My summary of our cheering performance: _____

_____

_____

_____

Coach's comments: _____

_____

_____

What I did well: _____

_____

_____

_____

Where I could have done better: _____

_____

_____

_____

Highlights of our cheering: _____

_____

_____

_____

Highlights of the game: _____

_____

_____

# Practice

Starting _____ until our next game on _____
                    Day & Date                                                               Day & Date

The main things we're focusing on this week are:

My focus this week is:

How I feel looking ahead:

What I think I can contribute to the squad this week:

My notes about this week's practice:

# Game Day

Game Date: _____  Game Time: _____

We played against: _____  Home ☐  Away ☐

Final Score: _____

My summary of our cheering performance: _____

_____

_____

_____

Coach's comments: _____

_____

_____

What I did well: _____

_____

_____

Where I could have done better: _____

_____

_____

Highlights of our cheering: _____

_____

_____

Highlights of the game: _____

_____

# Practice

Starting _____ until our next game on _____
　　　　　　　Day & Date　　　　　　　　　　　　　　　　　　　　　　　Day & Date

The main things we're focusing on this week are:



My focus this week is:



How I feel looking ahead:



What I think I can contribute to the squad this week:



My notes about this week's practice:

# Game Day

Game Date: _____     Game Time: _____

We played against: _____     Home ☐   Away ☐

Final Score: _____

My summary of our cheering performance:
_____
_____
_____

Coach's comments:
_____
_____

What I did well:
_____
_____
_____

Where I could have done better:
_____
_____
_____

Highlights of our cheering:
_____
_____
_____

Highlights of the game:
_____
_____

# Practice

Starting _____ until our next game on _____
　　　　　　Day & Date　　　　　　　　　　　　　　　　　　　Day & Date

The main things we're focusing on this week are:

My focus this week is:

How I feel looking ahead:

What I think I can contribute to the squad this week:

My notes about this week's practice:

# Game Day

Game Date: _____   Game Time: _____

We played against: _____   Home ☐   Away ☐

Final Score: _____

My summary of our cheering performance:
_____
_____
_____

Coach's comments:
_____
_____
_____

What I did well:
_____
_____
_____

Where I could have done better:
_____
_____
_____

Highlights of our cheering:
_____
_____
_____

Highlights of the game:
_____
_____

# Practice

Starting _____ until our next game on _____
               Day & Date                                                     Day & Date

The main things we're focusing on this week are:

My focus this week is:

How I feel looking ahead:

What I think I can contribute to the squad this week:

My notes about this week's practice:

# Game Day

Game Date: _____    Game Time: _____

We played against: _____    Home ☐   Away ☐

Final Score: _____

My summary of our cheering performance: _____

Coach's comments: _____

What I did well: _____

Where I could have done better: _____

Highlights of our cheering: _____

Highlights of the game: _____

# Practice

Starting _____ until our next game on _____
         Day & Date                                      Day & Date

The main things we're focusing on this week are:

My focus this week is:

How I feel looking ahead:

What I think I can contribute to the squad this week:

My notes about this week's practice:

# Game Day

Game Date: _____  Game Time: _____

We played against: _____  Home ☐   Away ☐

Final Score: _____

My summary of our cheering performance: _____

_____

_____

_____

Coach's comments: _____

_____

_____

What I did well: _____

_____

_____

Where I could have done better: _____

_____

_____

Highlights of our cheering: _____

_____

_____

Highlights of the game: _____

_____

# Practice

Starting _____ until our next game on _____
               Day & Date                                                          Day & Date

The main things we're focusing on this week are:

My focus this week is:

How I feel looking ahead:

What I think I can contribute to the squad this week:

My notes about this week's practice:

# Game Day

Game Date: _____  Game Time: _____

We played against: _____  Home ☐   Away ☐

Final Score: _____

My summary of our cheering performance:
_____
_____
_____
_____

Coach's comments:
_____
_____
_____
_____

What I did well:
_____
_____
_____
_____

Where I could have done better:
_____
_____
_____
_____

Highlights of our cheering:
_____
_____
_____
_____

Highlights of the game:
_____
_____

# Practice

Starting _____ until our next game on _____
              Day & Date                                                     Day & Date

The main things we're focusing on this week are:

My focus this week is:

How I feel looking ahead:

What I think I can contribute to the squad this week:

My notes about this week's practice:

# Game Day

Game Date: _____   Game Time: _____

We played against: _____   Home ☐   Away ☐

Final Score: _____

My summary of our cheering performance:
_____
_____
_____
_____

Coach's comments:
_____
_____
_____
_____

What I did well:
_____
_____
_____
_____

Where I could have done better:
_____
_____
_____
_____

Highlights of our cheering:
_____
_____
_____
_____

Highlights of the game:
_____
_____
_____

# Practice

Starting _____ until our next game on _____
             Day & Date                                                             Day & Date

The main things we're focusing on this week are:

My focus this week is:

How I feel looking ahead:

What I think I can contribute to the squad this week:

My notes about this week's practice:

# Game Day

Game Date: _____          Game Time: _____

We played against: _____          Home ☐   Away ☐

Final Score: _____

My summary of our cheering performance: _____

_____

_____

_____

Coach's comments: _____

_____

_____

What I did well: _____

_____

_____

Where I could have done better: _____

_____

_____

Highlights of our cheering: _____

_____

_____

Highlights of the game: _____

_____

# Practice

Starting _____ until our next game on _____
              Day & Date                                                      Day & Date

The main things we're focusing on this week are: _____

My focus this week is: _____

How I feel looking ahead: _____

What I think I can contribute to the squad this week: _____

My notes about this week's practice: _____

# Game Day

Game Date: _____  Game Time: _____

We played against: _____    Home ☐   Away ☐

Final Score: _____

My summary of our cheering performance:

_____
_____
_____

Coach's comments:

_____
_____
_____

What I did well:

_____
_____
_____

Where I could have done better:

_____
_____
_____

Highlights of our cheering: _____

_____
_____

Highlights of the game: _____

_____

# Practice

Starting _____ until our next game on _____
             Day & Date                                                             Day & Date

The main things we're focusing on this week are:

My focus this week is:

How I feel looking ahead:

What I think I can contribute to the squad this week:

My notes about this week's practice:

# Game Day

Game Date: _____     Game Time: _____

We played against: _____          Home ☐   Away ☐

Final Score: _____

My summary of our cheering performance:

_____
_____
_____

Coach's comments:

_____
_____
_____

What I did well:

_____
_____
_____

Where I could have done better:

_____
_____
_____

Highlights of our cheering:

_____
_____
_____

Highlights of the game:

_____
_____

# Practice

Starting _____ until our next game on _____
                Day & Date                                                                 Day & Date

The main things we're focusing on this week are:

My focus this week is:

How I feel looking ahead:

What I think I can contribute to the squad this week:

My notes about this week's practice:

What a season you've had!
You've used up 20 of your
worksheet sets.
There's one more after this page.
Use it to make as many
photocopies as you need
to complete your season.

# Game Day

Game Date: _____  Game Time: _____

We played against: _____  Home ☐   Away ☐

Final Score: _____

My summary of our cheering performance:

_____

_____

_____

Coach's comments:

_____

_____

What I did well:

_____

_____

Where I could have done better:

_____

_____

Highlights of our cheering:

_____

_____

Highlights of the game:

_____

# Practice

Starting _____ until our next game on _____
               Day & Date                                                      Day & Date

The main things we're focusing on this week are:

My focus this week is:

How I feel looking ahead:

What I think I can contribute to the squad this week:

My notes about this week's practice:

# My CHEERLEADING Season Memories

*Memories*

*Memories*

*Memories*

*Memories*

*Memories*

*Memories*

*Memories*

*Memories*

# About the Author

Karleen Tauszik writes books mostly for children ages 8 to 12. Her goal as an author is to help kids excel—not only in their sports but other areas of life as well. She is married to a professional ventriloquist and magician and they live in the Tampa Bay area.

Interested in other sports? You'll find My Season journals for all these sports:

>   My Baseball Season
>   My Softball Season
>   My Soccer Season
>   My Hockey Season
>   My Football Season
>   My Basketball Season
>   My Volleyball Season
>   My Cricket Season
>   My Rugby Season
>   My Netball Season

Besides these, Karleen has created dozens of other books for kids. See them all at her website, KarleenT.com. Ask a parent to sign up for her newsletter so they'll be the first to know about new books and special sales.

www.ingramcontent.com/pod-product-compliance
Lightning Source LLC
Chambersburg PA
CBHW081349070526
44578CB00005B/783